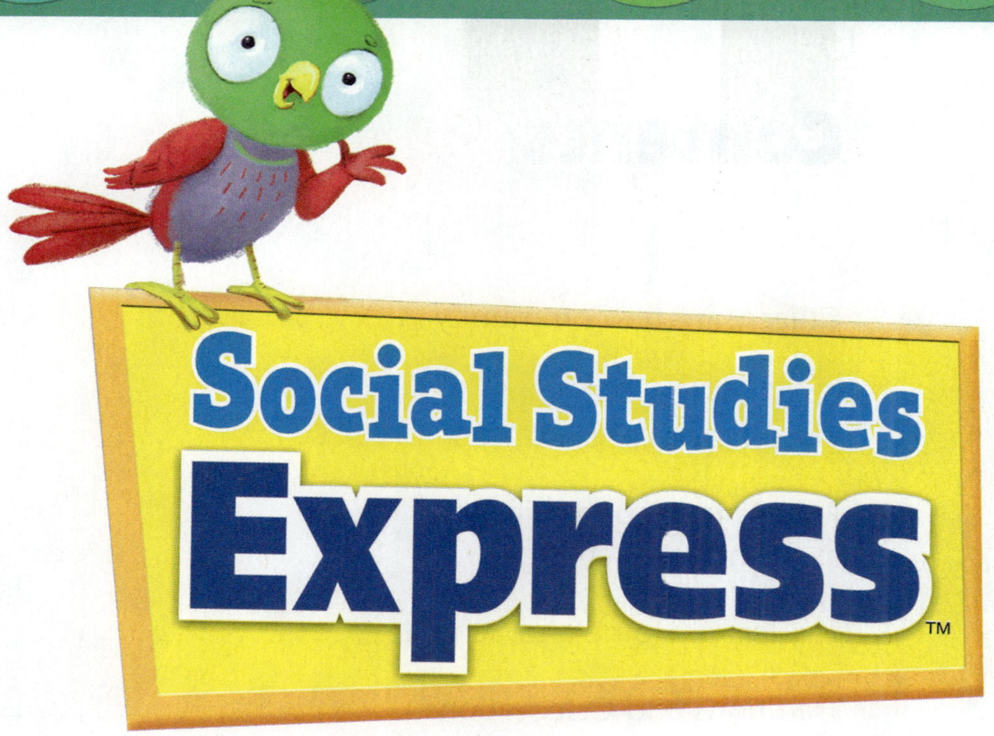

Wondering Why

Boston, Massachusetts • Chandler, Arizona • Glenview, Illinois • Upper Saddle River, New Jersey

PEARSON

ISBN-13: 978-0-328-79238-2
ISBN-10:   0-328-79238-1

4 5 6 7 8 9 10 V011 19 18 17 16 15

People (Culture)

Time (History)

Stuff (Economics)

Space (Geography)

Rules (Civics)

People (Culture)

Time (History)

Stuff (Economics)

Space (Geography)

Rules (Civics)

People (Culture)

Time (History)

Contents

Citizens in the Community

Objectives

- Define *community*.
- Describe how citizens in a community follow rules.
- Identify ways that citizens help others in the community and keep the community clean.
- Discuss good citizenship through the *Thinking Like a Citizen* lenses.

Make Connections You just talked about good citizenship. Describe what you do to show good citizenship.

Interactive Whiteboard Activity Write about one of the pictures you circled in the interactive whiteboard activity.

Watch and Discuss a Video Draw a picture to show a fire safety tip that the children learned on the field trip.

Describe the tip.

Create a Community Make a sign for the community that you created.

Thinking Like a Citizen Connection Copy the question you chose. Then write your answer.

Interactive Whiteboard Activity Choose one question from the activity. Draw a picture of it. Write about how it shows a good citizen.

The Spectacular Spectacles

Talk and Write About It Pick one question that you talked about. Write the answer.

Try on the Glasses Write about the lenses you picked. How did it feel to wear them?

Act It Out Draw a picture to show how you get along with others at home or school.

Make Your Own Spectacles Draw a picture of yourself with your spectacles on. Tell what you see when you wear them.

Questions to Talk or Write About Pick a question to answer from *The Spectacular Spectacles*. Then write your answer.

Rules and Responsibilities at Home and School

Objectives

- Define and explain the meanings of *rule, responsibility,* and *rights*.
- Identify rules, responsibilities, and rights at home and at school.
- Explain why we need rules.
- Discuss rules and responsibilities through the *Thinking Like a Citizen* lenses.

Make Connections Write a rule that you follow at home.

Watch and Discuss a Video Write a question that you have about the video on making rules.

Interactive Whiteboard Activity Draw a picture to show a responsibility you have at home or at school.

Interactive Whiteboard Activity Pick one picture from the activity. Write about it.

![Explore!]

Design a Rule Sign Write the rule from the sign you made.

Thinking Like a Citizen Connection Copy the question you chose to answer. Then write your answer.

Interactive Whiteboard Activity Draw a picture of yourself following a rule at home or in the community. Write a sentence about the rule.

Leaders at Home and School

Objectives
- Identify leaders at home, at school, and in the community.
- Describe what leaders do at home, school, and in the community.
- Discuss leaders at home and at school through the *Thinking Like a Citizen* lenses.

Make Connections Write the name of a leader at home. Describe what the leader does.

Learn!

Watch and Discuss a Video Write the name of a leader at school. Write one job that the leader does.

Interactive Whiteboard Activity Draw a picture of a leader in the community.

Write what the leader does to keep you safe.

Act It Out What was the hardest part about being a leader?
Write your answer.

Thinking Like a Citizen Connection Choose one of the questions you discussed. Copy the question and then write your answer.

Interactive Whiteboard Activity Choose one of the leaders from the activity. Describe what the leader does.

Keep Learning: Be a Leader Draw a picture of yourself as a leader. Write your job at the bottom of your picture.

Traditions and Celebrations

Objectives

- Identify elements that make up culture.
- Recognize that families and communities have different customs and traditions and different ways of celebrating.
- Explain that celebrations are ways to honor special people and events.
- Recognize that holidays are special days that honor people, events, or religious traditions.
- Discuss traditions and celebrations through the *Thinking Like a Citizen* lenses.

Make Connections Draw a picture of your family celebrating a special day. Use a piece of paper if you need more room.

Interactive Whiteboard Activity Describe how you or your family share your culture with others.

Interactive Whiteboard Activity Describe how you celebrate a tradition with your family.

Make a Classroom Cookbook Draw a cover for the classroom cookbook.

Make a Holiday or Celebration Card Write about your card. Why did you pick the holiday or celebration?

Thinking Like a Citizen Connection Copy the question you chose to answer. Then write your answer.

Interactive Whiteboard Activity Draw a picture that shows a part of culture that is not clothing, shelter, or food.

Interactive Whiteboard Activity Write about why we celebrate one of the holidays from the activity.

Why Can't I Say That?

Objectives
- Identify reasons why some words cannot be used at school.
- Understand different ways to deal with emotions such as anger and sadness instead of using hurtful words.

Make Connections You just talked about the lenses in *Why Can't I Say That?* Write about one of the lenses.

____

____

____

____

Talk and Write About It Write about one of the problems in the book.

____

____

Explore!

Try It Out Draw a picture to show how it felt when someone said words to you that hurt.

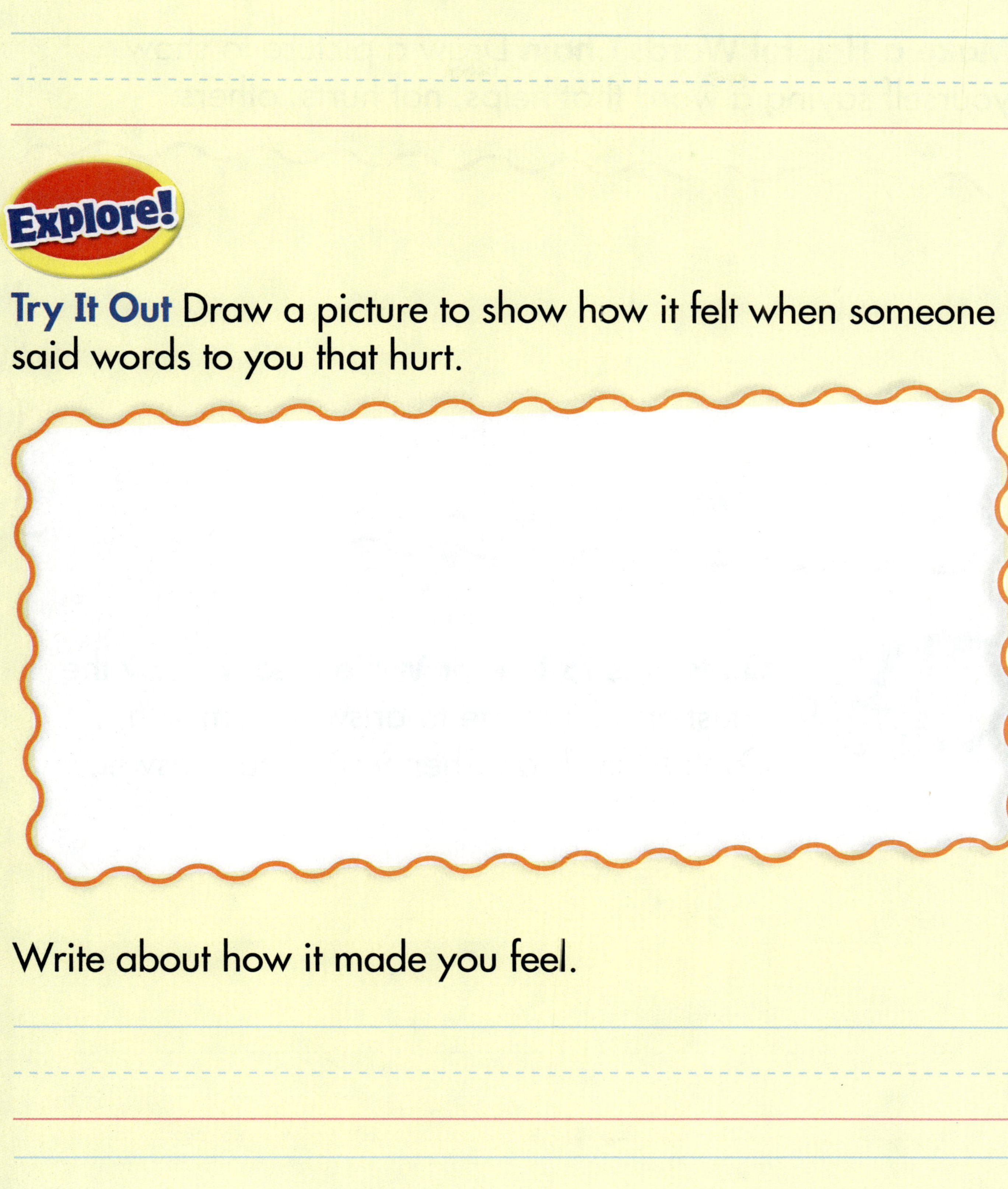

Write about how it made you feel.

Make a Helpful Words Chain Draw a picture to show yourself saying a word that helps, not hurts, others.

Questions to Talk or Write About Copy the question you chose to answer from *Why Can't I Say That?* Then write your answer.

Conflict and Cooperation

Objectives

- Define the terms *conflict* and *cooperation*.
- Identify the problems that can arise from conflict or when people do not cooperate.
- Explain how conflicts might be resolved in fair and just ways, and how they can be prevented through cooperation.
- Discuss conflict and cooperation through the *Thinking Like a Citizen* lenses.

Make Connections Draw a picture of a conflict in the first box. Draw a picture to show how it was solved in the second box. Use your own paper if you need more room.

Watch and Discuss a Video You just watched a video on what it means to cooperate. Write about how you cooperate at home or at school.

Interactive Whiteboard Activity Write about one of the problems in the activity. Tell how the children cooperated to solve the problem.

Find a Solution! Draw a picture. Show the best solution to the problem.

Write about why it is the best solution.

Thinking Like a Citizen Connection Choose one of the questions you discussed. Copy the question. Write your answer.

Identify the Conflict and Solution Write the conflict and solution from the video.

Make a Cooperation Day Badge Draw a badge to show that you cooperate with others.

Needs, Wants, and Choices

Objectives

- Define *needs* and *wants*, and identify basic human needs (food, water, clothing, shelter).
- Understand that humans work to earn money to meet their needs and wants.
- Understand how humans make choices about wants.
- Discuss needs and wants through the *Thinking Like a Citizen* lenses.

Get Ready!

Make Connections Draw a picture of your favorite food.

Write about the food you drew.

Make a Chart Draw a picture of a need and a want.

Write a sentence to tell why each is a need or a want.

Watch and Discuss a Video Write about a job you want when you grow up. Tell how working will help you get what you need and want.

Interactive Whiteboard Activity Write about a time when you made a choice.

Thinking Like a Citizen Connection Pick a question to answer. Then write your answer.

Interactive Whiteboard Activity Write about one want and one need.

Keep Learning: Go Shopping! Write about the toy or food you drew. Write about the choices you made.

Goods and Services

Objectives

- Define the terms *goods* and *services*, and explain how we use them in our daily lives.
- Understand that people trade goods and services at markets to get what they want and need.
- Discuss goods and services through the *Thinking Like a Citizen* lenses.

Make Connections Draw yourself doing a chore at home.

Watch and Discuss a Video Draw a good from the video.

Write about how the good gets to market.

Make a List of Goods and Services Write about a good or service that your family has bought on an errand.

Make a Farm to Table Flowchart Write about the food in your flowchart. How did it get from the farm to your table?

Thinking Like a Citizen Connection Copy the question you chose to answer. Then write your answer.

Interactive Whiteboard Activity Write about how goods and services are different.

Keep Learning: Act It Out Write the words *producer* and *consumer*. Did you like being the producer or consumer? Why?

Maps and Globes

Objectives

- Understand how globes and maps are alike and different.
- Identify the key elements of a map such as the map title, map key, symbols, and compass rose.
- Identify the direction words.
- Understand how to use directions on a map.
- Discuss maps and globes through the *Thinking Like a Citizen* lenses.

Make Connections Use direction words to describe the location of your desk or chair in the classroom.

Watch and Discuss a Video Draw a map of your bedroom.

Key

Describe the location of an object in your bedroom.

Interactive Whiteboard Activity Draw a map of your classroom. Draw a compass rose. Label it with the cardinal directions.

Key

Create an Imaginary Place Write about what you liked most about making the map of an imaginary place.

Thinking Like a Citizen Connection Copy the question you chose to answer. Then write your answer.

Interactive Whiteboard Activity Write about the location of your state in our country. Use cardinal directions and direction words.

Keep Learning Draw the route you drew on the map.

Land and Water

Objectives

- Describe the differences between land and water.
- Recognize how land and water are shown on maps and globes.
- Understand that people change the water and land to meet their needs.
- Discuss land and water through the *Thinking Like a Citizen* lenses.

Make Connections Draw and color a picture of land and water in your community.

Watch and Discuss a Video You just watched a video on land and water. Write about one kind of land and one kind of water.

Sing a Song Write the names of some of the continents and oceans. Use the words from the song to help you.

Make a Landscape Draw a picture of the landscape you made.

Write about the land and water in your landscape.

Thinking Like a Citizen Connection Copy the question you chose to answer. Then write your answer.

Interactive Whiteboard Activity Write the names of three oceans and three continents from the activity.

1. ______________________   1. ______________________

2. ______________________   2. ______________________

3. ______________________   3. ______________________

Keep Learning: Be a Mapmaker! Write about one landform or body of water from the map you made.

____

____

____

____

____

Why Do We Have to Learn This?

Objectives
- Identify the purpose of Presidents' Day.
- Ask and answer questions about the Presidents of the United States.

Make Connections Copy a question from the board. Write your answer to the question.

Question:

Answer:

Interactive Whiteboard Activity Write about what we celebrate on Presidents' Day.

Make a Poster Would you like to be president? Why or why not? Write your answer.

Make an Invitation Invite someone to your Presidents' Day celebration. Use words and pictures in your invitation.

Questions to Talk or Write About Pick a question to answer from *Why Do We Have to Learn This?* Then write your answer.

Life Then and Now

Objectives

- Understand the difference between past and present.
- Understand that some things have changed and others have stayed the same.
- Compare daily life, school, work, communication, and transportation in the past and present.
- Explain the difference between primary and secondary sources.
- Discuss the past and present through the *Thinking Like a Citizen* lenses.

Watch and Discuss a Video Draw a classroom from "then" and "now" in the boxes.

Then | Now

Interactive Whiteboard Activity Write about an object from the past, present, and future.

Past:

Present:

Future:

Explore!

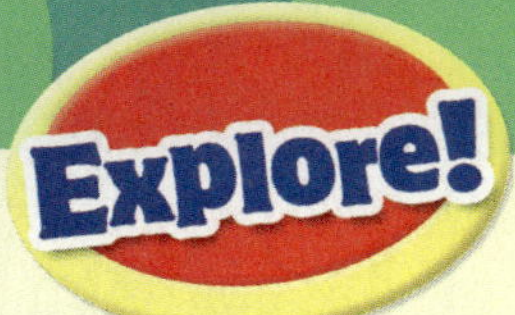

Interactive Whiteboard Activity Draw a picture from the activity. Show something from the past that we do not use today.

Write about what we use today.

Thinking Like a Citizen Connection Pick one of the questions you discussed. Copy the question. Then write your answer.

Interactive Whiteboard Activity Write about one thing we use now to communicate that we did not use in the past.

Keep Learning: Then and Now Write about what was alike and different on your poster.